It's OK to be Different
Colouring and Activity Book

A Celebration of Diversity and Kindness

This Book Belongs To

_____

It's OK to be Different
Colouring and Activity Book For Kids 6-8
A celebration of diversity and kindness

Written by Sharon Purtill
Based off the best selling picture book *It's OK to be Different.*

Published by Dunhill Clare Publishing - Ontario, Canada
Copyright© 2025 Dunhill Clare Publishing
dunhillclare@gmail.com

Illustrations by Tamara Piper

Paperback UK English Edition   ISBN: 978-1-990469-73-2

(NOTE: A US English Edition is available under ISBN: 978-1-990469-72-5)

Library and Archives Canada Cataloguing in Publication

be kind

We are all different

and wonderfully unique.

Do you know each and every person is different?

It's true!

If everyone looked and acted the same,
how would we know who was who?

Some kids love to swim

and some like to hike.

Some like to dance

and some love to bike.

We are all different.

Some kids love the colour blue
and some adore yellow.

Maybe pink is your favourite colour,
like this little fellow.

Some kids love building towers out of blocks.

Some kids enjoy wearing
different coloured socks!

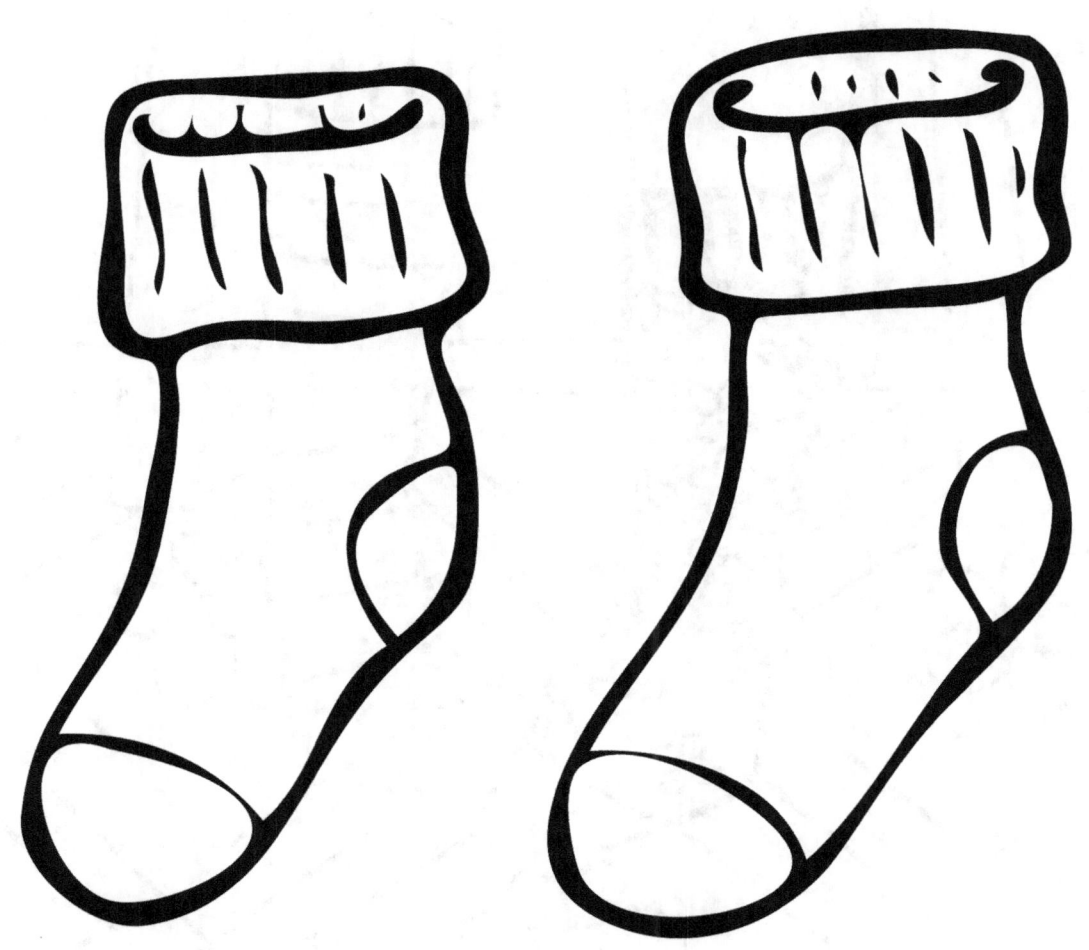

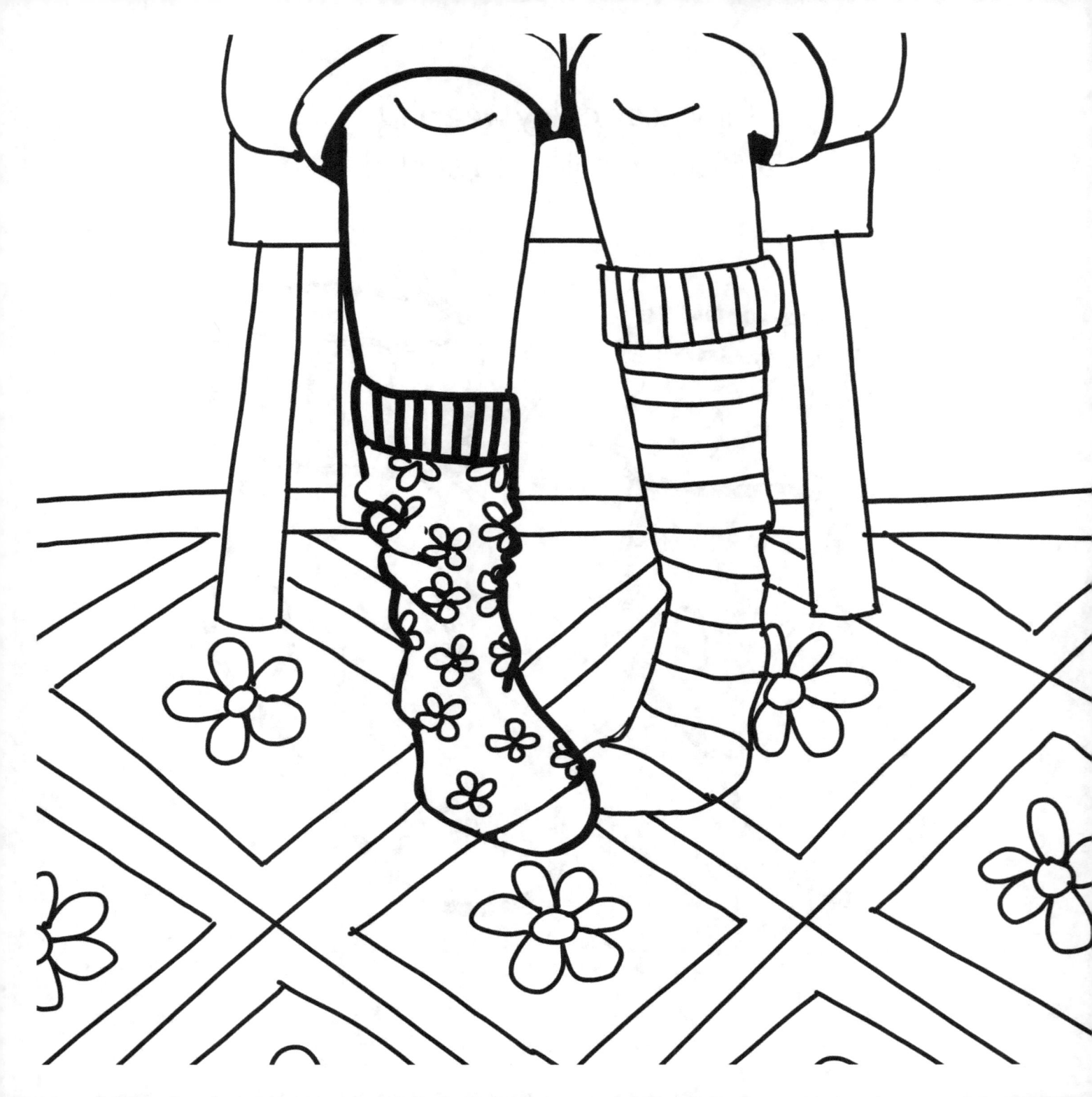

We are all different.

Some kids have blond hair and light coloured skin.
Some kids have dark hair and dark coloured skin.

How would you describe your own physical traits?

My hair is _____

My skin is _____

My eyes are _____

My height is _____

One of my unique characteristics is:

_____

Some kids are **big**

and some kids are small.

Some kids are short and others are tall!

Who is the tallest among your friends?

_____

Some kids get to ride in cool looking chairs.
They take the ramp while others take the stairs.

Who do you know
that uses a
wheelchair to
get around?

_____

Our skin, hair and size can be unique,
like what we believe, or how we speak.

Not every child is able to hear,
some use sign language so words are more clear.

Some are great
at sciences and maths

and some kids excel
on different paths.

Astronomy

Basketball

Running

Gymnastics

Skate Boarding

Perhaps playing sports
or music's
their thing.

Some kids play an
instrument, while
others can sing.

What do you excel at?

Music

Art

Dance

List a few of the things you are good at:

_____

_____

_____

Name something you'd like to learn more about:

_____

What could you learn from kids
who are different from you?

_____

_____

_____

What could you teach others?

_____

_____

We are
all different.

Sugars and sweets are not always a treat.
Some kids really need to watch what they eat.

If diabetic, their sugar can get too low or too high.

Some kids take medicine to help them get by.

YOU ARE
STRONGER
THAN YOU THINK

BELIEVE
in
YOURSELF

YOU ARE
BRAVER
THAN YOU KNOW

MAZE GAME

Draw a line through the maze to help Peter find his friend.

Peter

Some kids wear glasses that help
them to see. Some kids talk with an
accent that's different from me.

Some kids have glasses,
crutches, wheelchairs
and slings, but it's never
OK to make fun of
these things.

Empathy and compassion for others is key.

Some kids have struggles that
go beyond what we see.

How could you show empathy for someone?

_____

_____

_____

How could you show compassion to someone?

_____

_____

_____

Think about the last time you showed kindness.

Who did you show
kindness to?: _____

What kindness did you show them?

What inspired you to be kind at that moment?

How was your kindness received?

How did showing this person kindness make you feel?

Think about the last time someone was kind to you.

Who showed you
kindness?: _____

What kindness did they show you?

Why do you think this person showed you kindness?

How did their act of kindness make you feel?

How did you show appreciation for the kindness you received?

• SPREAD •
Kindness

Even though we don't all look, act
or sound alike, one thing is true.

Every child is an individual,
a person like YOU.

You should always be KIND to
those who are different from you.

Because to them,
YOU are different too.

Remember, it's OK to be different.
It's OK to be you!

You were made to be different.
You were made to be ... YOU.

What are some of the ways you could show yourself more compassion and love?

_____

_____

_____

_____

_____

_____

_____

Draw a self portrait in the frame below.

Draw the flag that represents
the country you were born in.

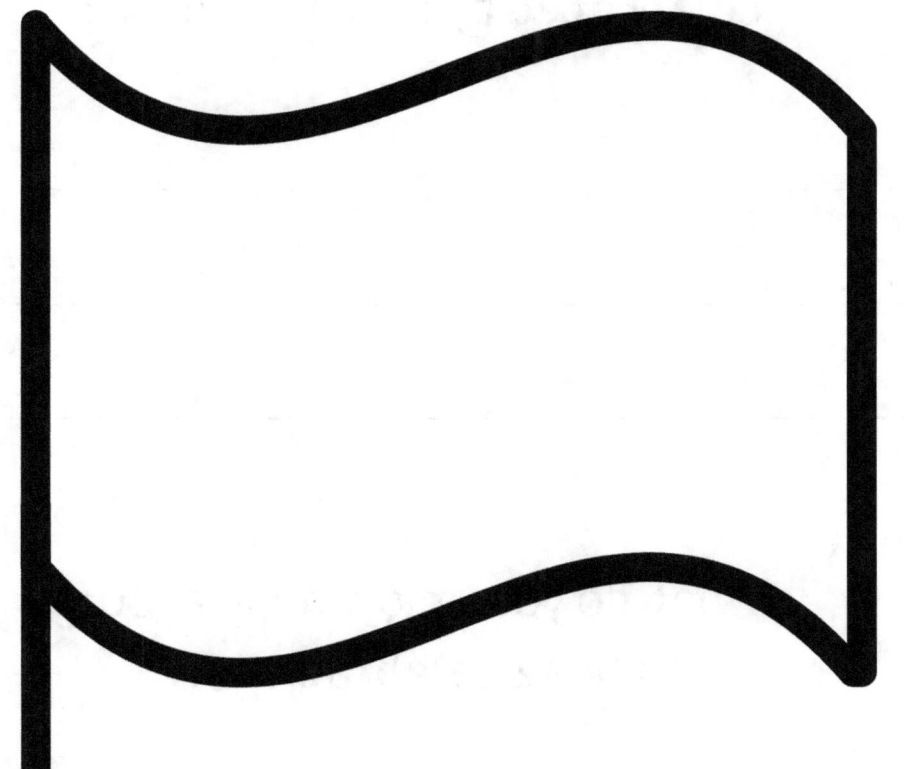

This flag represents the country of

_____

What holidays do you and your family celebrate together that may be different from those celebrated by other children?

_____

_____

_____

What do you enjoy most about these celebrations?

_____

_____

_____

When you ask others about themselves you may discover you have more in common than you thought. Here are some questions you can ask others:

Can you tell me about your family?

Do you have any pets at home?

What hobbies do you enjoy?

What is your greatest strength?

Is there anything you'd like to learn more about?

What makes you happy?   What makes you sad?

What would you like to do when you grow up?

The list of words below are hidden for you to find in the word search puzzle on the next page.

Can you find them all?

KIND   US

FRIEND   LEARN

DIVERSE   EMPATHY

GROW   COMPASSION

HELPFUL   DIFFERENT

Words can be horizontal, vertical or diagonal.

WORD SEARCH

C	C	D	I	V	E	R	S	E	G
D	O	E	H	O	L	B	Q	P	K
E	I	M	O	E	G	R	O	W	I
M	I	F	P	G	L	I	H	O	N
P	B	W	F	A	R	P	P	C	D
A	L	S	R	E	S	W	F	Y	W
T	E	S	I	D	R	S	A	U	S
H	A	R	E	Q	J	E	I	L	L
Y	R	M	N	A	N	C	N	O	M
Y	N	S	D	T	C	K	H	T	N

It's OK to be Different

Who do you know who is
different from you?

If you have noticed differences
maybe they have too.

What about them makes them
different from you?

And if you wanted to show them
kindness, what would you do?

We are all human and share many of the same characteristics. But, it's our differences that make us who we are.

I hope you always celebrate the uniqueness that is you!

Sharon Purtill

www.ingramcontent.com/pod-product-compliance
Lightning Source LLC
Chambersburg PA
CBHW081010120626
46546CB00010B/3094